The Dead Lecturer

The Dead Lecturer

Poems by

LeRoi Jones

GROVE PRESS, INC.   NEW YORK

Various poems in the present volume have appeared in the following publications: *American Negro Poetry, Beloit Poetry Journal, Beyond the Blues, Burning Deck, Evergreen Review, The Floating Bear, Fuck You/A Magazine of the Arts, Locus Solus, Massachusetts Review, The Nation, Niagara Frontier Review, Poetry, Set, The Seasons, Signal, Trobar, Village Voice, Yale Literary Magazine.*

Manufactured in the United States of America by The Book Press, Brattleboro, Vermont

Contents

The Dead Lecturer

For Edward Dorn

"In blackest day, In blackest night
No evil shall escape my sight!
Let those who worship evil's might
Beware my power . . .
Green Lantern's Light."

As a possible lover

Practices
silence, the way of wind
bursting
its early lull. Cold morning
to night, we go so
slowly, without
thought
to ourselves. (Enough
to have thought
tonight, nothing
finishes it. What
you are, will have
no certainty, or
end. That you will
stay, where you are,
a human gentle wisp
of life. Ah . . .)
                      practices
loneliness,
as a virtue. A single
specious need
to keep
what you have
never really
had.

Balboa, The Entertainer

It cannot come
except you make it
from materials
it is not
caught from. (The philosophers
of need, of which
I am lately
one,
      will tell you. "The People,"
(and not think themselves
liable
to the same
trembling flesh). I say now, "The People,
as some lesson repeated, now,
the lights are off, to myself,
as a lover, or at the cold wind.

Let my poems be a graph
of me. (And they keep
to the line, where flesh
drops off. You will go
blank at the middle. A
dead man.

      But
die soon, Love. If
what you have for
yourself, does not
stretch to your body's
end.
      (Where, without
preface,
music trails, or your fingers
slip
from my arm

A contract.   (for the destruction and
                      rebuilding of Paterson

Flesh, and cars, tar, dug holes beneath stone
a rude hierarchy of money, band saws cross out
music, feeling. Even speech, corrodes.
                                    I came here
from where I sat boiling in my veins, cold fear
at the death of men, the death of learning, in
cold fear, at my own. Romantic vests of same death
blank at the corner, blank when they raise their fingers

Criss the hearts, in dark flesh staggered so marvelous
are their lies. So complete, their mastery, of these
stupid niggers. Loud spics kill each other, and will not

make the simple trip to Tiffany's. Will not smash their stainless
heads, against the simpler effrontery of so callous a code as gain.

You are no brothers, dirty woogies, dying under dried rinds, in
        massa's
droopy tuxedos. Cab Calloways of the soul, at the soul's juncture,
        a
music, they think will save them from our eyes. (In back of the
        terminal

where the circus will not go. At the backs of crowds, stooped
        and vulgar
breathing hate syllables, unintelligible rapes of all that linger in
our new world. Killed in white fedora hats, they stand so mute
        at what

whiter slaves did to my fathers. They muster silence. They pray
        at the
steps of abstract prisons, to be kings, when all is silence, when all
is stone. When even the stupid fruit of their loins is gold, or
        something
else they cannot eat.

This is the clearing I once spoke of

The talk scared him. Left alone, with me,
at some water. (Suddenness of your mind,
because you will be saved. Stand there
counting deaths. My own, is what I wanted
you to say, Roi, you will die soon.)

                                    And
it went well, till evening, and the birds
fled. Their trees hanging empty at the
river. All of it a creation. More than
ideas. The simple elegant hand, a man
will extend. More than we can lose, and
still talk lovingly of "ourselves."

The brush sank behind its silence. This
was a jungle, dead children of thought.
We sat looking, and the wind changed
our fire, it was blue, and sang slowly.

Whose mind has this here? The way love
will move. I love you, I say that now
evenly, without emotion. Having
lost you. Or sitting, at the ruptured
threads of light. Wind and birds, spun
out over the water, silent or dead.

A Poem For Neutrals

A japanese neon landscape blinks
a constant film
of memory. His leaves, his hills
change in dumb perspective. Farmers
and Americans,
            say they are blue. Some natural phenomenon
some possible image
of what we shall call history. A jungle
of feeling. In their minds, the broken
tree, wet blood in the romantic's bulb. Our sudden
and misconceived beauty. Inept tenderness. (For
those long girls lay in darkness under our smell.
Those talkers who will not shut up
when the dawn comes. And stand in doorways
letting cold air blow in.
            It is a history of motive,
as secure as the economy
for these restless dwarfs
performing miracles for the blind. The wet ring
on their pants
the menace
of our education. It is not Dante,
nor Yeats. But the loud and drunken
pilgrim, I knew so well
in my youth. And grew to stone
waiting for the change.

2.

The calendar is memory. The dead roots
of the poet's brain. Yellow skin, black
skin, or the formless calm of compromise. They will not come
to see, or understand you. They will call you "murderer,"
as new songs for their young. The mountains

in your country, the flat skies of mine. (Except
by the oceans, the poor hate their shadows,
and force their agony to dance.

All night blue leaves ring
in Kyoto. And the windows of 5th street
scream.

An Agony. As Now.

I am inside someone
who hates me. I look
out from his eyes. Smell
what fouled tunes come in
to his breath. Love his
wretched women.

Slits in the metal, for sun. Where
my eyes sit turning, at the cool air
the glance of light, or hard flesh
rubbed against me, a woman, a man,
without shadow, or voice, or meaning.

This is the enclosure (flesh,
where innocence is a weapon. An
abstraction. Touch. (Not mine.
Or yours, if you are the soul I had
and abandoned when I was blind and had
my enemies carry me as a dead man
(if he is beautiful, or pitied.

It can be pain. (As now, as all his
flesh hurts me.) It can be that. Or
pain. As when she ran from me into
that forest.
                    Or pain, the mind
silver spiraled whirled against the
sun, higher than even old men thought
God would be. Or pain. And the other. The
yes. (Inside his books, his fingers. They
are withered yellow flowers and were never
beautiful.) The yes. You will, lost soul, say
'beauty.' Beauty, practiced, as the tree. The
slow river. A white sun in its wet sentences.

15

Or, the cold men in their gale. Ecstasy. Flesh
or soul. The yes. (Their robes blown. Their bowls
empty. They chant at my heels, not at yours.) Flesh
or soul, as corrupt. Where the answer moves too quickly.
Where the God is a self, after all.)

Cold air blown through narrow blind eyes. Flesh,
white hot metal. Glows as the day with its sun.
It is a human love, I live inside. A bony skeleton
you recognize as words or simple feeling.

But it has no feeling. As the metal, is hot, it is not,
given to love.

It burns the thing
inside it. And that thing
screams.

The pressures.

(Love twists
the young man. Having seen it
only once. He expected it
to be, as the orange flower
leather of the poet's book.
He expected
less hurt, a lyric. And not
the slow effortless pain
as a new dripping sun pushes
up out of our river.)
                    And
having seen it, refuses
to inhale. "It was a
green mist, seemed
to lift and choke
the town."

A Poem For Willie Best*

I

The face sings, alone
at the top
            of the body. All
flesh, all song, aligned. For hell
is silent, at those cracked lips
flakes of skin and mind
twist and whistle softly
as they fall.
            It was your own death
you saw. Your own face, stiff
and raw. This
without sound, or
movement. Sweet afton, the
dead beggar bleeds
yet. His blood, for a time
alive, and huddled in a door
way, struggling to sing. Rain
washes it into cracks. Pits
whose bottoms are famous. Whose sides
are innocent broadcasts
of another life.

---

* Willie Best was a Negro character actor whose Hollywood name was
Sleep'n'eat.

II

At this point, neither
front nor back. A point, the
dimensionless line. The top
of a head, seen from Christ's
heaven, stripped of history
or desire.
                    Fixed, perpendicular
to shadow. (even speech, vertical,
leaves no trace. Born in to death
held fast to it, where
the lover spreads his arms, the line
he makes to threaten Gods with history.
The fingers stretch to emptiness. At
each point, after flesh, even light
is speculation. But an end, his end,
failing a beginning.

2

A cross. The gesture, symbol, line
arms held stiff, nailed stiff, with
no sign, of what gave them strength.
The point, become a line, a cross, or
the man, and his material, driven in
the ground. If the head rolls back
and the mouth opens, screamed into
existence, there will be perhaps
only the slightest hint of movement—
a smear; no help will come. No one
will turn to that station again.

III

At a cross roads, sits the
player. No drum, no umbrella, even
though it's raining. Again, and we
are somehow less miserable because
here is a hero, used to being wet.
One road is where you are standing now
(reading this, the other, crosses then
rushes into a wood.
      5 lbs neckbones.
      5 lbs hog innards.
      10 bottles cheap wine.
           (The contents
of a paper bag, also shoes, with holes
for the big toe, and several rusted
knives. This is a literature, of
symbols. And it is his gift, as the
bag is.
    (The contents
again, holy saviours,
       300 men on horseback
       75 bibles
       the quietness
of a field. A rich
man, though wet through
by the rain.
     I said,
       47 howitzers
       7 polished horses jaws
       a few trees being waved
softly back under
the black night
      All This should be
invested.

IV

Where
ever,
      he has gone. Who ever
mourns
or sits silent
to remember

There is nothing of pity
here. Nothing
of sympathy.

V

This is the dance of the raised
leg. Of the hand on the knee
quickly.

   As a dance it punishes
speech. 'The house burned. The
old man killed.'

         As a dance it
is obscure.

VI

This is the song
of the highest C.
        The falsetto. An elegance
that punishes silence. This is the song
of the toes pointed inward, the arms swung, the
hips, moved, for fucking, slow, from side
to side. He is quoted
saying, "My father was
never a jockey,
        but
            he did teach me
            how to ride."

VII

The balance.

        (Rushed in, swarmed of dark, cloaks,
and only red lights pushed a message
to the street. Rub.

        This is the lady,
I saw you with.
This is your mother.
This is the lady I wanted
some how to sleep with.

        As a dance, or
our elegant song. Sun red and grown
from trees, fences, mud roads in dried out
river beds. This is for me, with no God
but what is given. Give me.

        Something more
than what is here. I must tell you
my body hurts.

The balance.

        Can you hear? Here
I am again. Your boy, dynamite. Can
you hear? My soul is moved. The soul
you gave me. I say, my soul, and it
is moved. That soul
you gave me.

        Yes, I'm sure
this is the lady. You
slept with her. Witness, your boy,
here, dynamite. Hear?

        I mean
can you?

The balance.
                    He was tired of losing. (And
his walking buddies tired
of walking.
          Bent slightly,
at the waist. Left hand low, to flick
quick showy jabs ala Sugar. The right
cocked, to complete,
                    any combination.
                              He was
tired of losing, but he was fighting
a big dumb "farmer."
                    Such a blue bright
afternoon, and only a few hundred yards
from the beach. He said, I'm tired
of losing.
          "I *got* ta cut 'cha."

VIII

A renegade
behind the mask. And even
the mask, a renegade
disguise. Black skin
and hanging lip.
                    Lazy
                    Frightened
                    Thieving
                    Very potent sexually
                    Scars
                    Generally inferior
                                    (but natural

rhythms.

His head is
at the window. The only
part
      that sings.

(The word he used
                    (we are passing St. Mark's place
                    and those crazy jews who fuck)
                                    to provoke

in neon, still useful
in the rain,
            to provoke
some meaning, where before
there was only hell. I said
silence, at his huddled blood.
                    It is an obscene invention.
                    A white sticky discharge.
                    "Jism," in white chalk

on the back of Angel's garage.
Red jackets with the head of
Hobbes staring into space. "Jasm"
the name the leader took, had it
stenciled on his chest.
                              And he sits
wet at the crossroads, remembering distinctly
each weightless face that eases by. (Sun at
the back door, and that hideous mindless grin.
                              (Hear?

Joseph To His Brothers

They characterize
their lives, and I
fill up
with mine. Fill up
with what I have, with what
I see (or
need. I make
no distinction. As blind men
cannot love too quiet beauty.

These philosophers
rein up
their boats. Bring
their gifts, weapons
to my door. As if
that, in itself,
was courage, or counting
science.

The story is a long one. Why
I am here like this. Why you
should listen, now, so late, and
weary at the night. Its
heavy rain
pushing
the grass flat.

                    It is here
somewhere. It grows
here. Answers. Questions. Noise
as stiff as silence. Silver quiet
beaten heavy under rains. So little
of this we remember. So few portions
of our lives, go on.

SHORT SPEECH TO MY FRIENDS

A political art, let it be
tenderness, low strings the fingers
touch, or the width of autumn
climbing wider avenues, among the virtue
and dignity of knowing what city
you're in, who to talk to, what clothes
—even what buttons—to wear. I address
                              / the society
                              the image, of
                              common utopia.

                              / The perversity
                              of separation, isolation,
after so many years of trying to enter their kingdoms,
now they suffer in tears, these others, saxophones whining
through the wooden doors of their less than gracious homes.
The poor have become our creators. The black. The thoroughly
ignorant.
          Let the combination of morality
and inhumanity
begin.

2.

Is power, the enemy? (Destroyer
of dawns, cool flesh of valentines, among
the radios, pauses, drunks
of the 19th century. I see it,
as any man's single history. All the possible heroes
dead from heat exhaustion
                    at the beach,
                    or hiding for years from cameras

only to die cheaply in the pages
of our daily lie.
                    One hero
has pretensions toward literature
one toward the cultivation of errors, arrogance,
and constantly changing disguises, as trucker, boxer,
valet, barkeep, in the aging taverns of memory. Making love
to those speedy heroines of masturbation. Or kicking literal evil
continually down filmy public stairs.

A compromise
would be silence. To shut up, even such risk
as the proper placement
of verbs and nouns. To freeze the spit
in mid-air, as it aims itself
at some valiant intellectual's face.

There would be someone
who would understand, for whatever
fancy reason. Dead, lying, Roi, as your children
came up, would also rise. As George Armstrong Custer
these 100 years, has never made
a mistake.

The end of man is his beauty

And silence
which proves / but
a referent
to my disorder.
                    Your world shakes

cities die
beneath your shape.

        The single shadow

at noon
like a live tree
whose leaves
are like clouds

Weightless soul
at whose love faith moves
as a dark and
withered day.

They speak of singing who
have never heard song; of living
whose deaths are legends
for their kind.

            A scream
gathered in wet fingers,
at the top of its stalk.

—They have passed
and gone
whom you thot your lovers

In this perfect quiet, my friend,
their shapes
are not unlike
night's

The politics of rich painters

is something like the rest
of our doubt, whatever slow thought
comes to rest, beneath the silence
of starving talk.
                    Just their fingers' prints
staining the cold glass, is sufficient
for commerce, and a proper ruling on
humanity. You know the pity
of democracy, that we must sit here
and listen to how he made his money.
Tho the catalogue of his possible ignorance
roars and extends through the room
like fire. "Love," becomes the pass,
the word taken intimately to combat
all the uses of language. So that learning
itself falls into disrepute.

2.

What they have gathered into themselves
in that short mean trip from mother's iron tit
to those faggot handmaidens of the french whore
who wades slowly in the narrows, waving her burnt out
torch. There are movies, and we have opinions. There are
regions of compromise so attractive, we daily long
to filthy our minds with their fame. And all the songs
of our handsome generation fall clanging like stones
in the empty darkness of their heads.
                              Couples, so beautiful
in the newspapers, marauders of cheap sentiment. So much *taste*
so little understanding, except some up and coming queer explain
cinema and politics while drowning a cigarette.

3.

They are more ignorant than the poor
tho they pride themselves with that accent. And
move easily in fake robes of egalitarianism. Meaning,
I will fuck you even if you don't like art. And are wounded
that you call their italian memories petit bourgeois.

                                           Whose death
will be Malraux's? Or the names Senghor, Price, Baldwin
whispered across the same dramatic pancakes, to let each eyelash
    flutter
at the news of their horrible deaths. It is a cheap game
to patronize the dead, unless their deaths be accountable
to your own understanding. Which be nothing nothing
if not bank statements and serene trips to our ominous country-
    side.
Nothing, if not whining talk about handsome white men. Nothing
if not false glamourous and static. Except, I admit, your lives
are hideously real.

4.

The source of their art crumbles into legitimate history.
The whimpering pigment of a decadent economy, slashed into
    life
as Yeats' mad girl plummeting over the nut house wall, her broken
knee caps rattling in the weather, reminding us of lands
our antennae do not reach.

And there are people in these savage geographies
use your name in other contexts
think, perhaps, the title of your latest painting
another name for liar.

Titles

My head
is a fine
tangle. My soul, a
quick note, settled
in the flesh.
                        There are so many lyrics,
so many
others
who will not understand.

I will say this to you tho,
It is not as if
there were
any more beautiful
way.

Style

the day roars black and empty
all dark. all light. all my
loves' deaths.
              to have been there, where
they talked tenderness. to have
seen it pass.
                to return to
what one felt
what one touched

and their nothing
grown to sounds
the deaf take for music.

Sex, like desire.

            (away from the streets. Flash
into pockets, the fingers' smell, deeply secret.
Each night, another rape. Young boys hide at the tops
of hills, near gas stations and breweries, waiting
to make the hit. It is not even love. Still, they
wait, and make believe
                        they are beautiful.

It could be me, even now. (So slow, I come to see
myself. To be at a point rusted in my dead child's
breast. Where the life is, all the flesh, to make
more than a silhouette, a breathless shadow counting
again, his change.

What is there? Where is it? Who is she? What can I
give myself, trade myself, to make me understand
myself? Nothing is ever finished. Nothing past. Each
act of my life, with me now, till death. Themselves,
the reasons for it. They are stones, in my mouth
and ears. Whole forests on my shoulders.

The invention of comics

I am a soul in the world: in
the world of my soul the whirled
light / from the day
the sacked land
of my father.

In the world, the sad
nature of
myself. In myself
nature is sad. Small
prints of the day. Its
small dull fires. Its
sun, like a greyness
smeared on the dark.

The day of my soul, is
the nature of that
place. It is a landscape. Seen
from the top of a hill. A
grey expanse; dull fires
throbbing on its seas.

The man's soul, the complexion
of his life. The menace
of its greyness. The
fire, throbs, the sea
moves. Birds shoot
from the dark. The edge
of the waters lit
darkly for the moon.

And the moon, from the soul. Is
the world, of the man. The man
and his sea, and its moon, and
the soft fire throbbing. Kind
death. O,
my dark and sultry
love.

A Poem For Democrats

the city rises

in color, our sad
ness, blanket this wood place, single drop
of rain, blue image of
someone's love.
Net of rain. Crystal ice
glass strings, smash
(on such repertoire of memory
as:
    baskets
    the long walk up harbor
    & the insistence, rain, as they build

City, is wicked. Not
this one, where I am, where they
still move, go to, out of
(transporting your loved one
across the line is death
by drowning.

Drowned love
hanged man, swung, cement on his feet.)
But

the small filth of the small mind
short structures of
newark, baltimore, cincinnati, omaha. Distress,
europe has passed we are alone. Europe
frail woman dead, we are alone

The Measure of Memory
(The Navigator

The presence of good
is its answer (at the curb
the dead white verb, horse
breathing white steam
in the air)
        Leaving, into the clocks
sad lovely lady fixed by words
her man
her rest
her fingers
her wooden house
set against the rocks
of our nation's
enterprise.

That we disappear
to dance, and dance
when we do,
badly.

And wield sentiment
like flesh
like the dumb man's voice
like the cold environment
of need. Or despair, a trumpet
with poison mouthpiece, blind player,
at the garden of least discernment; I
stagger, and remember / my own terrible
blankness and lies.

The boat's prow angled at the sun
Stiff foam and an invisible cargo
of captains. I buy injury, and decide
the nature of silence. Lines of speed
decay in my voice.

Footnote To A Pretentious Book

Who am I to love
so deeply? As against
a heavy darkness, pressed
against my eyes. Wetting
my face, a constant trembling
rain.

    A long life, to you. My friend. I
tell that to myself, slowly, sucking
my lip. A silence of motives / empties
the day of meaning.
                What is intimate
enough? What is
beautiful?

        It is slow unto meaning for
any life. If I am an animal, there
is proof of my living. The fawns
and calves
of my age. But it is steel that falls
as a thin mist into my consciousness. As a fine
ugly spray, I have made
some futile ethic
with.

    "Changed my life?" As the dead man
pacing at the edge of the sea. As
the lips, closed
for so long, at the sight
of motionless
birds.
    There is no one to entrust with
meaning. (These sails go by, these small
deadly animals.)

And meaning? These words?
Were there some blue expanse
of world. Some other
flesh, resting
at the roof
of the world . . .
                    you could say of me,
that I was truly
simpleminded.

Rhythm & Blues (1

(*for Robert Williams, in exile*)

The symbols hang limply
in the street. A forest of objects,
motives,
>   black steaming christ
>   meat wood and cars
>   flesh light and stars
>   scream each new dawn for

whatever leaves pushed from gentle lips
fire shouted from the loins of history
immense dream of each silence grown to punctuation
against the grey flowers of the world.

    I live against them, and hear them, and move
the way they move. Hanged against the night, so many
leaves, not even moving. The women scream tombs
and give the nights a dignity. For his heels
dragged in the brush. For his lips dry as brown wood. As
the simple motion of flesh whipping the air.

An incorrigible motive.
An action so secret it creates.
Men dancing on a beach.
Disappeared laughter erupting as the sea
erupts.
Controlled eyes seeing now all
there is
Ears that have grown
to hold their new maps
Enemies that grow
in silence
Empty white fingers
against the keys (a drunken foolish stupor

to kill these men
and scream "Economics," my God, "Economics"
for all the screaming women drunker still, laid out to rest
under the tables of nightclubs
under the thin trees of expensive forests
informed of nothing save the stink of their failure
the peacock insolence of zombie regimes
the diaphanous silence of empty churches
the mock solitude of a spastic's art.

"Love." My God, (after they
scream "Economics," these shabby personalities
the pederast anarchist chants against millions of
Elk-sundays in towns quieter than his. Lunches. Smells
the sidewalk invents, and the crystal music even dumb niggers
hate. They scream it down. They will not hear your jazz. Or
let me tell of the delicate colors of the flag, the graphic blouse
of the beautiful italian maiden. Afternoon spas
with telephone booths, Butterfingers, grayhaired anonymous
        trustees
dying with the afternoon. The people of my life
caressed with a silence that only they understand. Let their sons
make wild sounds of their mothers for your pleasure. Or
drive deep wedges in flesh / screaming birds of morning, at
their own. The invisible mountains of New Jersey, linger
where I was born. And the wind on that stone

2)

Street of tinsel, and the jeweled dancers
of Belmont. Stone royalty they tear down
for new buildings where fags invent jellies.

A tub, a slick head, and the pink houses waving
at the night as it approaches. A dead fish truck
full of porters I ran track with, effeminate blues singers, the
        wealth

of the nation transposed into the ring of my flesh's image. Grand dancers

spray noise and disorder in these old tombs. Liverwurst sand-wiches dry

on brown fenced-in lawns, unfinished cathedrals tremble with our screams.

Of the dozens, the razor, the cloth, the sheen, all speed adventure locked

in my eyes. I give you now, to love me, if I spare what flesh of yours

is left. If I see past what I feel, and call music simply "Art" and will

not take it to its logical end. For the death by hanging, for

the death by the hooded political murderer, for the old man dead in his

tired factory; election machines chime quietly his fraudulent faith.

For the well that marks the burned stores. For the deadly idiot of compromise

who shrieks compassion, and bids me love my neighbor. Even beyond the meaning

of such act as would give all my father's dead ash to fertilize their bilious

land. Such act as would give me legend, "This is the man who saved us

Spared us from the disappearance of the sixteenth note, the destruction

of the scale. This is the man who against the black pits of despair-ing genius

cried, "Save the Popular Song." For them who pat me in the huddle and do not

argue at the plays. For them who finish second and are happy they are Chinese,

and need not run those 13 blocks.

I am not moved. I will not move to save them. There is no "melody." Only the foot stomped, the roaring harmonies of need.

The
hand banged on the table, waved in the air. The teeth pushed
   against
the lip. The face and fingers sweating. "Let me alone," is praise
   enough
for these musicians.

3)

My own mode of conscience. And guilt, always the obvious
   connection.
They spread you in the sun, and leave you there, one of a kind,
   who
has no sons to tell this to. The mind so bloated at its own judg-
   ment. The
railing consequence of energy given in silence. Ideas whose sole
   place
is where they form. The language less than the act. The act so
   far beyond
itself, meaning all forms, all modes, all voices, chanting for safety.

I am deaf and blind and lost and will not again sing your quiet
   verse. I have lost
even the act of poetry, and writhe now for cool horizonless dawn.
   The
shake and chant, bulled electric motion, figure of what there will
   be
as it sits beside me waiting to live past my own meekness. My
   own
light skin. Bull of yellow perfection, imperfectly made, imperfectly
understood, except as it rises against the mountains, like sun
but brighter, like flame but hotter. There will be those
who will tell you it will be beautiful.

Crow Jane

"Crow Jane, Crow Jane, don't hold your head so high,
You realize, baby, you got to lay down and die."
—Mississippi Joe Williams

For Crow Jane
                    (Mama Death.

For dawn, wind
off the river. Wind
and light, from
the lady's hand. Cold
stuff, placed against
strong man's lips. Young gigolo's
of the 3rd estate. Young ruffians
without no homes. The wealth
is translated, corrected, a
dark process, like thought, tho
it provide a landscape
with golden domes.
                    'Your people
without love.' And life
rots them. Makes a silence
blankness in every space
flesh thought to be. (First light,
is dawn. Cold stuff
to tempt a lover. Old lady
of flaking eyes. Moon lady
of useless thighs.

Crow Jane's Manner.

                          Is some pilgrimage
to thought. Where she goes, in fairness,
"nobody knows." And then, without love,
returns to those wrinkled stomachs
ragged bellies / of young ladies
gone with seed. Crow
will not have. Dead virgin
of the mind's echo. Dead lady
of thinking, back now, without
the creak of memory.
                          Field is yellow. Fils dead
(Me, the last . . . black lip hung
in dawn's gray wind. The last,
for love, a taker, took my kin.

Crow. Crow. Where
you leave my
other boys?

Crow Jane In High Society.

                               (Wipes
her nose
on the draperies. Spills drinks
fondles another man's
life. She is looking
for alternatives. Openings
where she can lay all
this greasy talk
on somebody. Me, once. Now
I am her teller.
                      (And I tell
her symbols, as the grey movement
of clouds. Leave
grey movements
of clouds. Leave, always,
more.

Where is she? That she
moves without light. Even
in our halls. Even with
our laughter, lies, dead drunk
in a slouch hat famous king.
                            Where?

To come on so.

Crow Jane The Crook.

Of the night
of the rain, she
reigned, reined, her
fat whores and horse.

(A cloud burst,
and wet us. The mountain
split, and burned us. We thought
we were done.

                Jane.
Wet lady of no image. We
thought, you had left us. Dark
lady, of constant promise. We thought
you had gone.

2.

My heart is cast in bitter
metal. Condiments, spices
all the frustration of earth,
that has so much more desire

than resolution. Want than pleasure.
Oh, Jane. (Her boat bumps at the ragged
shore. Soul of the ocean, go out, return.
Oh, Jane, we thought you had gone.

The dead lady canonized.

                      (A thread
of meaning. Meaning light. The quick
response. To breath, or the virgins
sick odor against the night.

                      (A trail
of objects. Dead nouns, rotted faces
propose the night's image. Erect
for that lady, a grave of her own.

                      (The stem
of the morning, sets itself, on
each window (of thought, where it
goes. The lady is dead, may the Gods,

                      (those others
beg our forgiveness. And Damballah, kind father,
sew up
her bleeding hole.

Duncan spoke of a process

And what I have learned
of it, to repeat, repeated
as a day will repeat
its color, the tired sounds
run off its bones. In me, a balance.

Before that, what came easiest. From
wide poles, across the greenest earth,
eyes locked on, where they could live, and
whatever came from there, where the hand
could be offered, like Gideon's young troops
on their knees at the water.

                    I test myself,
with memory. A live bloody skeleton. Hung as softly
as summer. Sways like words' melody, as ugly as any
lips, or fingers stroking lakes, or flesh like a
white frightened scream.

What comes, closest, is
closest. Moving, there
is a wreck of spirit,
               a heap of broken feeling. What

was only love
or in those cold rooms,
opinion. Still, it made
color. And filled me
as no one will. As, even
I cannot fill
myself.

      I see what I love most and will not
leave what futile lies
I have. I am where there

is nothing, save myself. And go out to
what is most beautiful. What some noncombatant Greek
or soft Italian prince
would sing, "Noble Friends."
                              Noble Selves. And which one
is truly
to rule here? And
what country is this?

Audubon, Drafted

(for Linda)

It does not happen. That love, removes
itself. (I am leaving, Goodbye!
                  Removes
itself, as rain, hard iron rain
comes down, then stops. All those
eyes opened for morning, close with
what few hours given them. With tears,
or at a stone wall, shadows drag down.

I am what I think I am. You are what
I think you are. The world is the
one thing, that will not move. It is
made of stone, round, and very ugly.

If Into Love The Image Burdens

The front of the head
is the scarred cranium. The daisy
night, alone with its mills. Grumbling
through history, with its nest
of sorrow. I felt lost
and alone. The windows
sat on the street and smoked
in dangling winter. To autumn
from spring, summer's questions
paths, present to the head
and fingers. The shelf. The
rainbow. Cold knuckles rub against
a window. The rug. The flame. A woman
kneels against the sill. Each figure
halves silence. Each equation
sprinkles light.

Grey hats and eyes
for the photographed
trees. Grey stones and limbs
and a herd of me's.

Past, perfect.

Each correct color
not in nature, makes
us weep. Each inexpressible
idea. The fog lifts. The fog
lifts. Now falls. The fog
falls.

And nothing is done, or complete. No person
loved, or made better or beautiful. Came here
lied to, leave

the same. Dead boned talk
of history. Grandfathers skid
down a ramp of the night. Flame
for his talk, if it twists
like light on leaves.

Out past the fingers.
Out past the eyes.

I Substitute For The Dead Lecturer

*What is most precious, because
it is lost. What is lost,
because it is most
precious.*

They have turned, and say that I am dying. That
I have thrown
my life
away. They
have left me alone, where
there is no one, nothing
save who I am. Not a note
nor a word.

        Cold air batters
the poor (and their minds
turn open
like sores). What kindness
What wealth
can I offer? Except
what is, for me,
ugliest. What is
for me, shadows, shrieking
phantoms. Except
they have need
of life. Flesh
at least,
        should be theirs.

The Lord has saved me
to do this. The Lord
has made me strong. I
am as I must have

myself. Against all
thought, all music, all
my soft loves.

        For all these wan roads
I am pushed to follow, are
my own conceit. A simple muttering
elegance, slipped in my head
pressed on my soul, is my heart's
worth. And I am frightened
that the flame of my sickness
will burn off my face. And leave
the bones, my stewed black skull,
an empty cage of failure.

BLACK DADA NIHILISMUS

.   . Against what light

is false what breath
sucked, for deadness.
                        Murder, the cleansed

purpose, frail, against
God, if they bring him
                        bleeding, I would not

forgive, or even call him
black dada nihilismus.

The protestant love, wide windows,
color blocked to Mondrian, and the
ugly silent deaths of jews under

the surgeon's knife. (To awake on
69th street with money and a hip
nose. Black dada nihilismus, for

the umbrella'd jesus. Trilby intrigue
movie house presidents sticky the floor.
B.D.N., for the secret men, Hermes, the

blacker art. Thievery (ahh, they return
those secret gold killers. Inquisitors
of the cocktail hour. Trismegistus, have

them, in their transmutation, from stone
to bleeding pearl, from lead to burning
looting, dead Moctezuma, find the West

a grey hideous space.

2.

From Sartre, a white man, it gave
the last breath. And we beg him die,
before he is killed. Plastique, we

do not have, only thin heroic blades.
The razor. Our flail against them, why
you carry knives? Or brutaled lumps of

heart? Why you stay, where they can
reach? Why you sit, or stand, or walk
in this place, a window on a dark

warehouse. Where the minds packed in
straw. New homes, these towers, for those
lacking money or art. A cult of death,

need of the simple striking arm under
the streetlamp. The cutters, from under
their rented earth. Come up, black dada

nihilismus. Rape the white girls. Rape
their fathers. Cut the mothers' throats.
Black dada nihilismus, choke my friends

in their bedrooms with their drinks spilling
and restless for tilting hips or dark liver
lips sucking splinters from the master's thigh.

Black scream
and chant, scream,
and dull, un
earthly

hollering. Dada, bilious
what ugliness, learned
in the dome, colored holy
shit (i call them sinned

or lost
      burned masters
              of the lost
                       nihil German killers
                              all our learned

art, 'member
what you said
money, God, power,
a moral code, so cruel
it destroyed Byzantium, Tenochtitlan, Commanch
                         (got it, *Baby!*

For tambo, willie best, dubois, patrice, mantan, the
bronze buckaroos.

        For Jack Johnson, asbestos, tonto, buckwheat,
        billie holiday.

          For tom russ, l'overture, vesey, beau jack,

(may a lost god damballah, rest or save us
against the murders we intend
against his lost white children
black dada nihilismus

A Hip Kitty

I wanted to kiss
dead middleclass visitors. Young colored girls
with slides, and casual polka dots.

                                     The term would be

a country
home, full of murderers
and illegality. The social order
listening quietly
from the bedroom.
                I would drive them there
                and back. Or pay their way
                on the train.

A Guerrilla Handbook

In the palm
the seed
is burned up
in the wind.
        In their rightness
the tree trunks are socialists
leaves murder the silence and are brown
and old when they blow to the sea.
                    Convinced

of the lyric. Convinced
of the man's image (since
he will not look at substance
other than his ego. Flowers, grapes
the shadows of weeds, as the weather
is colder, and women walk
with their heads down.
              Silent political rain
against the speech
of friends. (We love them
trapped in life, knowing no way out
except description. Or black soil
floating in the arm.
          We must convince the living
          that the dead
          cannot sing.

Green Lantern's Solo

A deep echo, of open fear: the field drawn in
as if to close, and die, in the old man's eyes
as if to shut itself, as the withered mouth of
righteousness beats its gums on the cooling day.

                    As if to die
                    without knowing life.
                    Having lived, when
                    he did (an old stout God
                    in the spent bones
                    of his dignity. No screams
                    break his wooden lips
                    His urine scatters
                    as steel, which will fall
                    on any soft thing
                    you have. (Murder

                    is speaking of us.

I break and run, or hang back and hide
having been killed by wild beasts in my young wife's
sleep. Having been torn into small echoes of lie, or surrounded
in dim rooms by the smelly ghosts of wounded intellectuals. Old
    science majors
                    whose mothers were brilliant understudys
            or the famous mistress of a benevolent gangster.
    Some mysterious comment on the world at the birth
of the word. Some mysterious jangle of intellects bent on the
    crudeness
of any death so perfectly ignorant as ours.
                    My friend, the lyric poet,
                who has never had an orgasm. My friend,
            the social critic, who has never known society,
        or read the great italian liars, except his father
who calls the whitehouse nightly, asking for hideous assignments.

My friend who has thrown himself against the dignity of all
human flesh
yet beats at its image, as if he was the slow intellect who thought
up
God.
      No, Nigger, no, blind drunk in SantaSurreal's beard. Dead
hero
for our time who would advance the nation's economy by poking
holes
in his arms. As golden arms build a forest of loves, and find only
the heavy belly breath of ladies whispering their false pregnancies
through the
phone. The stagnant image of bats sailing out of their mouths as
they
shape the syllable of revenge. Let me say it is Love, but never
feeling.
It is knowledge, but never perfection, or something as stupidly
callous
as beauty.

2.

So important a silence as their lives, dwindled, rusted, corrupted
away. As the port, where smoke rises for the poor french sailor
and his indian whore. There are bones, which still clog those blue
soft seas, and give a human history to nature. Can you understand
that nothing is free! Even the floating strangeness of the poet's
head
the crafted visions of the intellect, *named, controlled,* beat and
erected
to work, and struggle under the heavy fingers of art. What valley,
what
mountain, what eagle or afternoon, is not fixed or changed under
our feet
or eyes? What man unremoved from his meat's source, can
continue

to believe totally in himself? Or on the littered sidewalks of his
        personal
history, can continue to believe in his own dignity or intelligence.
Except the totally ignorant
who are our leaders.
                Except the completely devious
                who are our lovers.
                        No man except a charlatan
                        could be called "Teacher," as

big birds will run off from their young
if they follow too closely, or the drowned youths at puberty
who did not allow that ritual was stronger than
their mother's breasts.

The completely free are the completely innocent, of which
no thing I know can claim: despite the dirty feet
of our wise men, their calm words hung in a line, from city
to city: despite the sickening courage or useless honesty
of men who claim to love each other and resolve their lives
as four letter words: despite the rightness, the strength
the brilliance and character, the undeniable idiocy of poets
like Marx and Rousseau.
                What we have created, is ourselves
                as heroes, as lovers, as disgustingly
                evil. As Dialogues with the soul, with
                the self, Selves, screaming furiously
                to each other. As the same fingers
                touch the same faces, as the same
                mouths close on each other. The killed
                is the killer, the loved the lover
and the islands of mankind have grown huge to include all life,
all lust, all commerce and beauty. Each idea a reflection of itself
and all the ideas men have ever had. Truth, Lie, so close they
        defy
inspection, and are built into autonomy by naive fools,

who have no wish for wholeness or strength. Who cannot but
     yearn
for the One Mind, or Right, or call it some God, a thing beyond
themselves, some thing toward which all life is fixed, some static,
irreducible, constantly correcting, dogmatic economy
                       of the soul.

The dance.
                (held up for me by
an older man. He told me how. Showed
me. Not steps, but the fix
of muscle. A position
for myself: to move.

Duncan
told of dance. His poems
full of what we called
so long for you to be. A
dance. And all his words
ran out of it. That there
was some bright elegance
the sad meat of the body
made. Some gesture, that
if we became, for one blank moment,
would turn us
into creatures of rhythm.

I want to be sung. I want
all my bones and meat hummed
against the thick floating
winter sky. I want myself
as dance. As what I am
given love, or time, or space
to feel myself.

The time of thought. The space
of actual movement. (Where they
have taken up the sea, and
keep me against my will.) I said, also,
love, being older or younger
than your world. I am given
to lying, love, call you out
now, given to feeling things
I alone create.

And let me once, create
myself. And let you, whoever
sits now breathing on my words
create a self of your own. One
that will love me.

WAR POEM

The battle waxed (battle wax, good night!
    Steep tumors of the sea's energy
    shells, shells, gold lights under the tree's
    cover.)

           In spring the days explode
           In spain old cuckolds watch their wives
           and send their money to America.

           Straw roofs, birds, any thing we have not
           got. Destroyed before it got here. *Battle,*
           an old dead flower she put on her breast.

           Shells crush the beach. Are crushed
           beneath her feet. Wait for night,
           and the one soldier will not mind us
           sitting here, listening to the familiar
           water, scatter in the shadows.

Political Poem

Luxury, then, is a way of
being ignorant, comfortably
An approach to the open market
of least information. Where theories
can thrive, under heavy tarpaulins
without being cracked by ideas.

(I have not seen the earth for years
and think now possibly "dirt" is
negative, positive, but clearly
social. I cannot plant a seed, cannot
recognize the root with clearer dent
than indifference. Though I eat
and shit as a natural man. (Getting up
from the desk to secure a turkey sandwich
and answer the phone: the poem undone
undone by my station, by my station,
and the bad words of Newark.) Raised up
to the breech, we seek to fill for this
crumbling century. The darkness of love,
in whose sweating memory all error is forced.

Undone by the logic of any specific death. (Old gentlemen
who still follow fires, tho are quieter
and less punctual. It is a polite truth
we are left with. Who are you? What are you
saying? Something to be dealt with, as easily.
The noxious game of reason, saying, "No, No,
you cannot feel," like my dead lecturer
lamenting thru gipsies his fast suicide.

Snake Eyes

That force is lost
which shaped me, spent
in its image, battered, an old brown thing
swept off the streets
where it sucked its
gentle living.
                    And what is meat
to do, that is driven to its end
by words? The frailest gestures
grown like skirts around breathing.
                                        We take

unholy risks to prove
we are what we cannot be. For instance,

I am not even crazy.

A Poem For Speculative Hipsters

He had got, finally,
to the forest
of motives. There were no
owls, or hunters. No Connie Chatterleys
resting beautifully
on their backs, having casually
brought socialism
to England.
        Only ideas,
and their opposites.
                Like,
        he was *really*
        nowhere.

Dichtung

A torn body, correspondent

of extreme cold. Altitude
or thought, colliding as an image
of
moving water, time, the slip

of simple life. It is matter, after all,
that is corrupted, not
spirit. After all, it is spirit
that is corrupted
not matter.
    The role given,
mashed into protein
grace. A lifted arm
in shadow. A lifted thinking
banging silently
in the darkness.
      I fondle what
I find
of myself. Of you
what I understand.
      Trumpets of slow weather.
      Love blends
      in season.

Valéry As Dictator

Sad. And it comes
tomorrow. Again, gray, the streaks
of work
shedding the stone
of the pavement, dissolving
with the idea
of singular endeavor. Herds, the
herds
of suffering intelligences
bunched,
and out of
hearing. Though the day
come to us
      in waves,
            sun, air, the beat
of the clock.
         Though I stare at the radical
world,
      wishing it would stand still.
               Tell me,
and I gain at the telling.
Of the lie, and the waking
against the heavy breathing
of new light, dawn, shattering
the naive cluck
of feeling
        What is tomorrow
that it cannot come
         today?

The Liar

What I thought was love
in me, I find a thousand instances
as fear. (Of the tree's shadow
winding around the chair, a distant music
of frozen birds rattling
in the cold.

       Where ever I go to claim
my flesh, there are entrances
of spirit. And even its comforts
are hideous uses I strain
to understand.

       Though I am a man
who is loud
on the birth
of his ways. Publicly redefining
each change in my soul, as if I had predicted
them,

    and profited, biblically, even tho
    their chanting weight,

           erased familiarity
           from my face.

               A question I think,

an answer; whatever sits
counting the minutes
till you die.

    When they say, "It is Roi
    who is dead?" I wonder
    who will they mean?